How do Graphics Cards operate? Exploring GPU Technology

The Untold Story of Digital Minds and Technological Wonders

Sharon smiths

Table of contents

Introduction

Technology has always been humanity's relentless pursuit to push boundaries, defy limits, and create the extraordinary. Among its crowning achievements lies an invention that has quietly revolutionized everything from entertainment to scientific discovery—the graphics card. This seemingly humble piece of hardware is the unsung hero behind the vibrant worlds of modern gaming, the dazzling precision of cinematic visual effects, and the mind-bending calculations fueling artificial intelligence. It's a masterpiece of design and function, a digital marvel with the power to turn raw data into awe-inspiring reality. Yet, for all its contributions, the true genius of GPU technology remains an enigma to most.

The purpose of this book is to unveil the mysteries of graphics cards, offering readers a guided journey through their intricate design, evolution, and profound impact on the modern world. This is not just a technical guide but a story—an exploration of how GPUs have become the lifeblood of industries far beyond gaming. By breaking down their complex architecture into easily digestible insights, this book aims to empower you with a deeper appreciation for the unseen forces driving technological innovation.

To truly understand GPUs, we must first glance back at their origins. The history of graphics cards is a tale of relentless progress, born from the early days of computing when basic two-dimensional images ruled the screen. From the primitive VGA adapters of the 1980s to the transformative introduction of 3D acceleration in the 1990s, each decade brought exponential leaps in capability. What once struggled to render a handful of pixels now effortlessly produces billions, creating lifelike simulations that blur the line between virtual and real.

But why should you, as a reader, care about understanding GPU technology? The answer lies in its ever-expanding influence. GPUs are no longer confined to the realm of gamers or developers. They're at the forefront of breakthroughs in medicine, powering real-time diagnostics and complex genetic research. They're the engines behind cryptocurrency mining, driving an entire digital economy. They're reshaping industries, unlocking new possibilities in fields as diverse as architecture, space exploration, and autonomous vehicles. In essence, to understand GPUs is to understand the future—one where innovation is limited only by the scope of imagination.

This book invites you to join a journey of discovery, where the technical becomes tangible, and the abstract becomes awe-inspiring. Together, we'll uncover the story of GPUs: their birth, evolution, and the limitless potential they hold to shape our world. Whether you're a tech enthusiast, a student of engineering, or simply someone curious about the inner workings of the technology you use daily, this is your opportunity to delve deep into the world of graphics cards and emerge with a newfound sense of wonder.

Chapter 1: The Evolution of Graphics Cards

In the beginning, computers were little more than glorified calculators, designed to process raw data and solve complex equations. Visual representation was an afterthought, and the concept of computer graphics barely existed. Early machines like the ENIAC and UNIVAC relied solely on numerical outputs, leaving users to interpret rows of blinking lights or columns of printed numbers. But as technology advanced, so did the need for a more intuitive interface—one that could transform cold data into something visually meaningful. This necessity gave birth to the early days of computer graphics, a field that would revolutionize the way humans interacted with machines.

In the 1960s, the first sparks of computer graphics emerged in research labs. These pioneers envisioned a future where computers could not only calculate but also visualize. The earliest attempts were rudimentary at best—simple line drawings displayed on cathode-ray tube (CRT) monitors. Ivan Sutherland's groundbreaking program, Sketchpad, was a turning point. Released in 1963, Sketchpad allowed users to draw geometric shapes directly on a screen, an innovation that laid the foundation for modern graphical user interfaces (GUIs).

By the 1970s, the computer graphics industry began to take shape. Companies like Tektronix and Evans & Sutherland developed specialized hardware for rendering vector graphics, primarily for use in military simulations and scientific research. These systems, though revolutionary, were prohibitively expensive, limiting their reach to governments and elite institutions. Meanwhile, video game developers were experimenting with rudimentary graphics, introducing the world to blocky spaceships and pixelated aliens on arcade machines like Atari's Pong and Space Invaders. Though primitive by today's standards, these games captivated audiences and demonstrated the immense potential of interactive graphics.

The 1980s saw the rise of personal computing, a development that would forever change the trajectory of computer graphics. IBM introduced its first PC, and companies like Apple and Commodore followed suit, each vying to bring affordable, user-friendly machines into homes and offices. However, these early PCs were limited in their graphical capabilities, often displaying only text or crude monochrome images. To bridge the gap, manufacturers began developing dedicated graphics adapters, such as IBM's Color Graphics Adapter (CGA) and Hercules Graphics Card, which offered users the ability to display color and create simple visual designs.

As personal computers gained popularity, so did the demand for more immersive and visually appealing experiences. The late 1980s saw the introduction of Video Graphics Array (VGA) technology, which supported higher resolutions and a broader color palette. VGA became a standard, paving the way for a new era in computer graphics. Around the same time, the first 3D graphics experiments were conducted in research labs, hinting at the possibilities of rendering objects with depth and realism.

These early innovations were just the beginning. What started as a quest to enhance user interaction with machines had sparked a revolution in how humans perceive and engage with digital environments. From the monochrome screens of the past to the vibrant displays of today, the evolution of computer graphics set the stage for the development of specialized hardware that would forever change the landscape of technology—the graphics card.

The journey of graphics cards, from rudimentary tools to the powerhouses we know today, has been marked by groundbreaking milestones. Each innovation not only elevated the capabilities of GPUs but also redefined how we interact with technology. Understanding these key developments provides a clearer picture of how modern graphics cards evolved to handle complex visual tasks with breathtaking efficiency.

In the early 1990s, the emergence of 2D acceleration was a pivotal moment. Graphics cards like the S3 Graphics' S3 86C911 introduced hardware that could handle 2D tasks such as drawing windows, text, and basic shapes, offloading these duties from the CPU. This breakthrough allowed for smoother graphical interfaces, marking the first step toward dedicated graphics processing.

The mid-1990s witnessed a revolution with the advent of 3D acceleration. Companies like 3dfx Interactive released the iconic Voodoo Graphics card in 1996, specifically designed to render three-dimensional environments in real time. Gamers could now experience dynamic lighting, texture mapping, and smooth frame rates, ushering in an era where gaming began to push the boundaries of graphical realism. The Voodoo's impact was so profound that it established a new standard, prompting other companies to enter the burgeoning 3D graphics market.

By the late 1990s, NVIDIA emerged as a key player, introducing the GeForce 256 in 1999, hailed as the world's first GPU. Unlike its predecessors, the GeForce 256 integrated a hardware transform and lighting (T&L) engine, enabling it to handle complex mathematical operations required for rendering 3D scenes. This innovation drastically improved performance, allowing for richer graphics in both games and professional applications. NVIDIA's bold branding of the GeForce 256 as a GPU (Graphics Processing Unit) cemented the term in the tech lexicon.

The early 2000s brought another game-changing development: programmable shaders. ATI Technologies, later acquired by AMD, launched the Radeon 9700 in 2002, the first graphics card to support fully programmable pixel and vertex shaders. This breakthrough allowed developers to create more intricate and realistic visual effects, from lifelike water reflections to detailed character animations. Programmable shaders marked a shift toward greater flexibility and creativity in game design.

The mid-2000s saw the rise of multi-GPU technology, spearheaded by NVIDIA's SLI (Scalable Link Interface) and ATI's CrossFire. These systems allowed users to link multiple graphics cards together, significantly boosting performance. For gamers and professionals working with demanding applications like 3D rendering or video editing, multi-GPU setups provided an unprecedented level of power and efficiency.

In 2006, NVIDIA's release of CUDA (Compute Unified Device Architecture) introduced a paradigm shift. CUDA transformed GPUs into general-purpose computing platforms capable of handling tasks beyond graphics, such as scientific simulations, machine learning, and cryptocurrency mining. This innovation opened up new avenues for GPU applications, solidifying their role as essential tools across various industries.

Another defining milestone came in 2018 with the introduction of real-time ray tracing technology. NVIDIA's RTX 20 series was the first to feature dedicated ray tracing cores, which simulate the behavior of light in real-time, producing hyper-realistic shadows, reflections, and lighting effects. This advancement bridged the gap between pre-rendered CGI and real-time graphics, setting a new benchmark for visual fidelity.

In parallel, AMD introduced its RDNA architecture, which emphasized efficiency and scalability, offering competitive performance at various price points. AMD's innovations pushed the market forward, ensuring healthy competition and continuous progress.

The evolution of graphics cards has been shaped by these key milestones, each building upon the last to deliver the stunning graphical experiences we enjoy today. From the humble beginnings of 2D acceleration to the cutting-edge capabilities of ray tracing, the journey of GPU development underscores the relentless pursuit of visual perfection in the digital age.

Chapter 2: Understanding GPU Architecture

The GPU and CPU are two distinct powerhouses in modern computing, each designed for specialized tasks. At first glance, they may seem similar—both are processors crucial to the operation of a computer. However, their underlying architectures and purposes reveal striking differences, making each uniquely suited to its role.

A CPU, or Central Processing Unit, is often referred to as the "brain" of a computer. It is designed for general-purpose tasks, excelling in sequential processing and handling a variety of instructions one step at a time. CPUs typically have a few high-performance cores that prioritize speed and efficiency in tasks such as running operating systems, managing software, and processing data. These cores are highly versatile, allowing the CPU to switch between different types of tasks rapidly.

In contrast, a GPU, or Graphics Processing Unit, is specifically engineered for parallel processing, the key to rendering complex images and graphics efficiently. Instead of a few powerful cores like the CPU, a GPU contains thousands of smaller, more specialized cores. These cores work simultaneously, processing multiple data streams in parallel, which is ideal for tasks that require handling vast amounts of data at once, such as rendering 3D graphics, processing video, or running machine learning algorithms.

The fundamental difference lies in how these two processors handle workloads. The CPU is optimized for low-latency tasks that require quick decision-making and logic. It shines in scenarios where a series of instructions must be completed in a specific order, like running a word processor, managing file systems, or performing calculations in spreadsheets. On the other hand, the GPU thrives in high-throughput environments, where massive amounts of similar calculations need to be done simultaneously. Rendering a video game, for example, requires processing millions of pixels and calculating the behavior of light, shadows, and textures—all tasks perfectly suited for the parallel structure of a GPU.

This divergence in design also extends to their physical structures. CPUs typically have larger, more complex control units and cache memory to manage intricate tasks efficiently. GPUs, meanwhile, allocate more of their resources to arithmetic logic units (ALUs) for processing large datasets. The result is a processor that sacrifices flexibility for sheer computational power in specific areas.

The rise of GPUs has not only transformed gaming and entertainment but has also revolutionized industries like scientific research, artificial intelligence, and cryptocurrency mining. In AI, for instance, GPUs accelerate the training of neural networks by quickly processing the vast amounts of data needed to teach machines how to recognize patterns and make decisions. Similarly, in scientific simulations, GPUs enable researchers to model complex systems, from molecular structures to astrophysical phenomena, with incredible speed and accuracy.

Understanding the unique strengths of GPUs compared to CPUs offers insight into why both are essential components in modern computing. Together, they form a symbiotic relationship, with the CPU acting as a master controller, delegating intensive, data-heavy tasks to the GPU. This dynamic duo ensures that computers operate with both precision and power, driving the innovations that shape our digital world.

At the heart of every graphics card lies a meticulously crafted symphony of components, each playing a pivotal role in its performance. These elements work together in harmony, transforming raw data into stunning visuals and enabling complex computational tasks. To truly understand how a graphics card operates, we must dissect its core components and explore their distinct functions.

CUDA Cores are the workhorses of a modern GPU, akin to the neurons in a brain. These cores handle the bulk of parallel processing, enabling the graphics card to perform millions of simultaneous calculations. Short for Compute Unified Device Architecture, CUDA cores are designed by NVIDIA to execute tasks like rendering 3D environments, processing intricate shaders, and even accelerating non-graphics tasks such as AI and scientific simulations. Each CUDA core may be relatively simple on its own, but when grouped by the thousands, their collective power becomes unparalleled.

Streaming Multiprocessors (SMs) serve as the organizational hubs of the GPU, grouping CUDA cores into manageable clusters. Each SM contains its own set of CUDA cores, memory, and control logic, allowing it to process multiple tasks simultaneously. SMs are designed for maximum efficiency, enabling the GPU to handle diverse workloads, from rendering video game graphics to performing real-time ray tracing. They distribute tasks across the GPU, ensuring that every core operates at peak performance.

Memory, or VRAM (Video Random Access Memory), is the storage powerhouse of the graphics card. Unlike traditional system RAM, VRAM is optimized for rapid data access, essential for storing and retrieving textures, frame buffers, and other graphical data. Its role is crucial; without sufficient VRAM, the GPU would constantly need to fetch data from the slower system memory, resulting in lag and reduced performance. VRAM's high-speed capabilities ensure seamless rendering of high-resolution textures and smooth gameplay, even in the most demanding scenarios.

To sustain the immense computational load, **power supply and cooling mechanisms** are indispensable. GPUs require a significant amount of electrical power, especially during intensive tasks like gaming or rendering. Modern graphics cards often come with dedicated power connectors to meet these demands. However, with great power comes great heat. To prevent overheating, GPUs rely on advanced cooling systems, ranging from traditional air coolers with fans and heatsinks to more sophisticated liquid cooling solutions. These mechanisms ensure that the GPU remains at an optimal temperature, maintaining performance and prolonging its lifespan.

At the center of task coordination is **the Gigathread Engine**, the unsung hero of the GPU. This engine manages the scheduling and distribution of threads across the streaming multiprocessors. It ensures that each thread block is assigned to the appropriate SM and that all tasks are executed efficiently. The Gigathread Engine plays a crucial role in balancing workloads, minimizing bottlenecks, and maximizing the GPU's computational throughput.

Together, these core components form the backbone of a graphics card, each contributing to its ability to deliver breathtaking visuals and perform complex computations. By understanding their roles, we gain a deeper appreciation for the technological marvel that powers our digital experiences.

Chapter 3: The Graphics Rendering Pipeline

In the world of computer graphics, the journey from a raw 3D model to a beautifully rendered image is a meticulous and highly structured process, guided by what's known as the graphics rendering pipeline. This intricate series of steps transforms abstract mathematical data into the vivid, lifelike visuals we see on screens. At the heart of this process lies a key stage: converting objects from **model space to world space**, followed by **vertex transformation and triangle assembly**. Let's unravel this journey.

Imagine a digital cowboy hat, meticulously crafted from a mesh of thousands of vertices, each defined by X, Y, and Z coordinates in a local coordinate system known as model space. In this context, the origin (0, 0, 0) is typically placed at the center of the object, making it easy to design and manipulate the hat in isolation. However, to situate this hat within a broader virtual scene—perhaps resting on a wooden table in a sunlit saloon—it must be translated into world space. This step repositions the object's vertices relative to the global scene, determining where the hat sits in relation to other objects, like the table or a nearby lantern.

The transition from model space to world space begins with a simple yet powerful instruction: adding the position of the object's origin in world space to each vertex coordinate in model space. For the cowboy hat, this means updating all 14,000 vertices to reflect their new positions in the shared world coordinate system. This process, though computationally intense, is optimized by leveraging **SIMD (Single Instruction, Multiple Data)**, where a single instruction is applied simultaneously across all vertices. This allows for rapid transformations, even in scenes containing thousands of objects and millions of vertices.

Once the vertices are positioned in world space, the next stage is **vertex transformation**. This step applies additional calculations to account for rotation, scaling, and perspective. For example, if the hat is slightly tilted or appears smaller due to distance from the camera, these adjustments are incorporated through matrix multiplications. Each transformation matrix—whether for translation, rotation, or scaling—is meticulously applied to ensure the object's visual accuracy within the scene.

After the transformations, the process advances to **triangle assembly**, where the individual vertices are grouped into triangles, the fundamental building blocks of 3D graphics. These triangles define the surface of the object, giving it shape and structure. For the cowboy hat, the assembly of thousands of interconnected triangles forms a seamless mesh, ready for further stages like shading and texturing.

This seamless progression from model space to world space, followed by vertex transformation and triangle assembly, exemplifies the precision and efficiency of the graphics rendering pipeline. It's a testament to the marvels of modern computing, where millions of calculations converge to create dynamic, immersive visual experiences.

As the graphics rendering pipeline progresses, the carefully transformed and assembled triangles undergo a crucial phase: **rasterization and pixel shading**. This is where the abstract geometric data becomes a vivid, pixelated image, bringing virtual worlds to life. Let's dive into the magic of how GPUs handle lighting, textures, shadows, and advanced rendering techniques like ray tracing.

Rasterization is the bridge between geometry and pixels. Once the triangles of a 3D model are mapped to screen space, the GPU determines which pixels (or fragments) on the screen correspond to each triangle. This process involves breaking down the triangles into a grid of fragments, each representing a potential pixel. The GPU works at astonishing speeds, calculating billions of fragments per second to ensure even the most complex scenes are accurately depicted.

However, raw fragments alone don't create the stunning visuals we've come to expect. This is where **pixel shading** steps in, breathing life into each fragment. Pixel shaders, small programs executed by the GPU, calculate the final color of each pixel by considering multiple factors: the object's material, its texture, and the scene's lighting. For instance, a cowboy hat might have a rough leather texture, rich brown hues, and subtle highlights from a nearby lantern. Pixel shading ensures these details come together seamlessly, giving the hat its realistic appearance.

Lighting plays a pivotal role in achieving realism. **Diffuse lighting** simulates how light scatters when it hits a rough surface, creating soft, even illumination. **Specular lighting** adds sharp highlights, mimicking the way light reflects off shiny surfaces. Shadows, calculated in tandem, anchor objects to their environment, enhancing depth and spatial relationships.

Textures further enrich the scene by overlaying detailed images onto the 3D models. Instead of crafting every tiny wrinkle or grain of wood through geometry, textures efficiently provide these details. By mapping high-resolution images onto the surfaces of triangles, GPUs create intricate visuals without overwhelming computational resources.

Despite these advancements, traditional rasterization has its limitations, particularly when rendering reflections, refractions, or complex light interactions. This is where **advanced rendering techniques** like **ray tracing** revolutionize the process. Ray tracing simulates the behavior of light as it travels through a scene, calculating how rays bounce, refract, or get absorbed. This results in breathtaking realism, capturing effects like accurate reflections in a glass window or the subtle interplay of light in a dimly lit room.

Unlike rasterization, which approximates lighting based on predefined models, ray tracing computes every interaction of light in real-time. For example, the gleam on a polished table, the way shadows soften at their edges, or the glow of sunlight filtering through a dusty saloon window—all are brought to life with unparalleled accuracy. While traditionally resource-intensive, modern GPUs equipped with **ray tracing cores** make these effects more accessible, pushing the boundaries of visual fidelity.

From rasterization to pixel shading and the leap to advanced techniques like ray tracing, GPUs continually redefine what's possible in digital imagery. This relentless pursuit of realism turns virtual scenes into cinematic masterpieces, captivating audiences and immersing them in worlds that blur the line between fiction and reality

Chapter 4: SIMD and SIMT Explained

SIMD (Single Instruction, Multiple Data) is a concept that allows a processor to execute the same operation simultaneously on multiple data points. It's a parallel processing technique that significantly boosts computational efficiency, particularly when working with large datasets. In simpler terms, SIMD enables the GPU to perform the same operation on multiple pieces of data, like transforming several vertices at once, rather than processing each one individually.

For example, imagine a scene where we need to transform the vertices of a 3D cowboy hat. Each vertex represents a point in 3D space that needs to undergo a series of transformations, like scaling, rotating, or translating, in order to be properly displayed on screen. If each vertex were processed individually, it would take much longer to complete the transformation for the entire object.

But with SIMD, the same transformation is applied simultaneously to all vertices, saving time and processing power. The GPU's parallel architecture allows it to execute the same instruction (like rotating or scaling) on multiple data points (the vertices of the cowboy hat) in a single cycle. This is particularly useful in graphics, where large numbers of vertices must be processed quickly for complex models, enabling a more fluid and realistic rendering experience.

Practical Example: Transforming the Vertices of a Cowboy Hat

Let's dive into the example of transforming the vertices of a cowboy hat using SIMD. In this case, imagine that the cowboy hat is made up of hundreds or even thousands of vertices in 3D space. Each vertex contains X, Y, and Z coordinates that define its position in space.

To transform these vertices, the GPU applies a mathematical operation to each one, such as rotating the hat by a certain angle or scaling it to make it larger or smaller. With SIMD, rather than performing these transformations one vertex at a time, the GPU executes the same transformation instruction on multiple vertices simultaneously.

Let's say we need to rotate the hat by 45 degrees around the Y-axis. Using SIMD, the GPU can apply this rotation matrix to a group of vertices in parallel. Each vertex will undergo the same transformation, but all at once, significantly speeding up the process. This parallel processing technique is particularly useful when dealing with large models, like the cowboy hat, that require transformations to many vertices at once.

In summary, SIMD allows GPUs to perform complex calculations on large datasets much faster by applying the same operation across multiple data points in parallel. In the context of graphics, this means transforming thousands of vertices in the blink of an eye, enabling real-time rendering of intricate 3D models like the cowboy hat with minimal delay. This efficiency is a cornerstone of modern GPU technology, ensuring that even the most detailed and complex scenes can be rendered quickly and realistically.

SIMT (Single Instruction, Multiple Threads) is an evolution of SIMD (Single Instruction, Multiple Data) that further enhances parallel processing by not only allowing multiple pieces of data to be processed simultaneously, but also by enabling multiple threads to execute the same instruction simultaneously. The key difference between SIMT and SIMD is that, in SIMT, each thread operates on a different piece of data, but all threads in a group follow the same instruction path at the same time.

Whereas SIMD focuses on executing the same operation on multiple pieces of data at once (like transforming multiple vertices), SIMT takes this a step further by treating each thread as a unit of execution, processing several threads at once and enabling highly parallel operations for complex tasks. In modern GPUs, this is the underlying model that allows for thousands of threads to work in parallel on various tasks such as shading, vertex processing, and ray tracing.

Warp Divergence and Its Impact on Performance

In the SIMT model, threads are organized into groups known as *warps*. A warp consists of 32 threads that are executed simultaneously by a single instruction unit in the GPU. All threads in a warp start by executing the same instruction. However, if threads within the same warp begin to diverge and take different execution paths (e.g., due to conditional statements like "if" clauses in code), this is referred to as **warp divergence**.

Warp divergence significantly impacts performance because the GPU has to execute the different paths in a serialized manner, rather than in parallel. For example, if half the threads in a warp need to execute one path of code and the other half need to execute a different path, the GPU will have to process these paths sequentially, first executing one set of threads and then executing the other, instead of running both paths simultaneously. This reduces the efficiency of the SIMT model, as it forces the hardware to wait for the divergent paths to complete before it can continue with the next instruction.

In real-world applications, especially in complex rendering tasks and simulations, warp divergence can cause a noticeable slowdown in performance. GPUs are optimized to minimize divergence, but in certain situations, such as in complex shading algorithms or when handling conditional branching, it can be hard to avoid. As a result, developers must be mindful of how they structure their programs to minimize these divergent branches and maximize the parallel execution capabilities of the GPU.

Barrier Synchronization and Thread Efficiency

Barrier synchronization is another important concept in the context of SIMT. In multi-threaded execution, threads often need to cooperate, sharing data and resources, which can lead to dependencies between threads. Barrier synchronization is a mechanism that ensures threads reach certain points in their execution at the same time, preventing some threads from advancing too far ahead of others and causing inconsistencies.

In a SIMT model, a barrier can be set to synchronize threads across warps or within a single warp. This is particularly useful when threads need to share data or complete certain calculations before proceeding to the next stage of execution. Without synchronization, threads might access incomplete data or resources, leading to errors or suboptimal performance.

However, synchronization comes with its own challenges. While barriers can ensure proper coordination, they can also introduce delays, as threads are forced to wait for others to reach the synchronization point. This can decrease overall throughput, especially if many threads are waiting on a single thread or warp to catch up. For efficient execution, it's crucial to balance synchronization points to avoid unnecessary waiting and ensure that threads can keep processing as much as possible without being held back.

In summary, SIMT offers a significant improvement over SIMD by enabling threads to execute the same instruction simultaneously, but it comes with its own set of challenges. Warp divergence can slow down performance, as the GPU is forced to handle threads that diverge down different paths. Similarly, barrier synchronization, while essential for coordinating threads, can introduce waiting times that reduce efficiency. To fully harness the power of SIMT, developers must carefully consider how to minimize divergence and optimize synchronization, ensuring that the GPU can process as many threads as possible in parallel and maintain high performance in rendering tasks and complex computations.

Chapter 5: Applications Beyond Gaming

GPU Use in Bitcoin Mining

In the early days of Bitcoin, miners used CPUs (central processing units) to validate transactions and create new blocks for the blockchain. However, as the network grew, the difficulty of these calculations increased significantly. CPU-based mining soon became impractical, as it could no longer keep up with the increasing computational demands. The solution came in the form of GPUs (graphics processing units), which, with their ability to handle massive parallel workloads, quickly became the new standard for cryptocurrency mining.

A GPU is designed to handle thousands of threads in parallel, making it far more efficient than a CPU at solving the cryptographic puzzles required for mining. While CPUs might excel at handling complex sequential tasks, GPUs are optimized for executing many tasks simultaneously, which is exactly what mining requires. As miners began to realize the power of GPUs, they quickly adopted them, and this shift led to the widespread use of GPUs in Bitcoin and other cryptocurrency mining operations.

SHA-256 Algorithm and Hash Calculations

At the heart of Bitcoin mining is the **SHA-256 algorithm** (Secure Hash Algorithm 256-bit), which is a cryptographic hash function. Bitcoin miners use SHA-256 to solve a complex mathematical puzzle that involves finding a hash value that satisfies certain conditions. The SHA-256 algorithm takes an input, processes it through multiple rounds of hashing, and produces a 256-bit output (the hash). The puzzle miners are trying to solve is essentially finding a specific hash value that matches the desired target, and they do this by continuously altering the input with small changes, called **nonce**values, until they find a solution.

Because the SHA-256 algorithm involves running the same series of operations repeatedly on different pieces of data, it is highly parallelizable. Each "thread" of the GPU can work on calculating a hash at the same time, allowing for thousands, or even millions, of potential hashes to be tested every second. The more hashes that are tested, the higher the chances of finding the correct one, which results in a successful block and a reward of newly minted Bitcoin.

This parallelism is what makes GPUs such an attractive option for Bitcoin miners. Unlike CPUs, which perform better on tasks requiring strong single-threaded performance, GPUs can execute the same operation across many data points simultaneously, drastically speeding up the mining process.

Why GPUs Were Initially Ideal for Mining

The primary reason that GPUs were initially ideal for Bitcoin mining lies in their **parallel processing architecture**. Unlike CPUs, which are optimized for general-purpose computing and sequential processing tasks, GPUs are specialized hardware designed for handling the highly parallel workloads of graphics rendering. They contain hundreds or even thousands of smaller cores that can work on different parts of a task simultaneously. This architecture makes GPUs well-suited to solving the cryptographic puzzles required for mining.

When Bitcoin mining first started, it was based on the principle of "proof-of-work," where miners had to find a solution to a cryptographic puzzle. The process of trying different hash values is computationally expensive, and while a CPU could technically perform the calculations, it was far too slow to be practical for serious miners. In contrast, the GPU's architecture allowed for far more efficient parallel computation, significantly accelerating the hashing process. Miners could now test many possible hash values in a fraction of the time it would take with a CPU, giving them a competitive edge.

Furthermore, GPUs were already widely used for gaming and high-performance computing, meaning they were readily available and relatively affordable for miners. This made the transition to GPU-based mining straightforward, and soon, mining farms and independent miners alike began using GPUs to mine Bitcoin and other cryptocurrencies. The rise of GPU-based mining led to the creation of mining rigs—custom-built setups using multiple GPUs that could work in parallel to maximize hash rates and mining efficiency.

As mining difficulty continued to rise, however, GPUs were eventually surpassed by more specialized hardware like **ASICs (Application-Specific Integrated Circuits)**, which are designed specifically for mining and offer even greater performance and efficiency than GPUs. Nonetheless, GPUs continue to be widely used for mining other cryptocurrencies that rely on algorithms that are better suited to parallel processing, such as Ethereum.

In summary, GPUs revolutionized Bitcoin mining by offering unparalleled parallel processing power, making them far more efficient than CPUs for the repetitive and parallelizable task of solving cryptographic puzzles. Their ability to test thousands or millions of hash values in parallel made them an ideal tool for miners, and they played a pivotal role in the growth and development of the cryptocurrency ecosystem. Even as the industry has evolved and new technologies like ASICs have emerged, GPUs remain integral to many other areas of mining and computational tasks.

Artificial Intelligence and Machine Learning

The use of GPUs has expanded far beyond gaming and cryptocurrency mining, as they have become essential tools in the fields of **artificial intelligence (AI)** and **machine learning (ML)**. These fields involve handling vast amounts of data and performing complex calculations, tasks that GPUs excel at due to their parallel processing capabilities. While CPUs can handle tasks that require high single-threaded performance, GPUs shine when it comes to parallel workloads—exactly what AI and ML require for training and deploying models.

Machine learning involves feeding algorithms vast amounts of data and allowing them to learn patterns or make decisions based on that data. The more data and computations involved, the longer it takes to process and train models. However, with the power of GPUs, many AI researchers and data scientists have experienced significant reductions in training time, allowing models to be trained faster and more efficiently. The combination of powerful cores and high memory bandwidth means that GPUs can handle the simultaneous computations needed to process complex datasets with ease.

Deep learning algorithms, a subset of machine learning, are particularly well-suited to GPUs due to their reliance on matrix multiplications and other parallelizable operations. This has led to GPUs being adopted by tech giants like Google, Facebook, and OpenAI, who leverage them to train massive neural networks. The advancement in AI has truly been propelled by the parallel computation power of GPUs, which can simultaneously perform a variety of tasks—an essential feature when working with the huge datasets required for deep learning.

Introduction to Tensor Cores

To further enhance their usefulness in machine learning, NVIDIA developed **Tensor Cores**, specialized hardware built into their Volta and Turing architectures, designed specifically for AI and machine learning tasks. Tensor Cores accelerate the matrix multiplications and convolutions that are essential to training deep neural networks.

Tensor Cores are highly optimized for performing the type of matrix operations that occur in many deep learning algorithms. The performance boost from Tensor Cores can be enormous—up to 12 times faster than standard GPU cores for specific AI workloads. These cores use **mixed-precision arithmetic**, which allows them to process both lower-precision data (such as half-precision floating-point numbers) and higher-precision data (single-precision or double-precision) with remarkable efficiency. This innovation means that neural network training can be performed at lightning speeds, allowing researchers to experiment with larger datasets and more complex models, all while maintaining accuracy.

Tensor Cores have proven indispensable for deep learning frameworks like TensorFlow, PyTorch, and MXNet. These frameworks are widely used by researchers and companies to build and train machine learning models. By utilizing Tensor Cores, the time it takes to train models has been dramatically reduced, enabling rapid advancements in AI capabilities, from computer vision to natural language processing.

Neural Networks and Matrix Multiplications

Neural networks are composed of layers of interconnected nodes, often referred to as neurons, that process and transform data as it passes through. One of the core operations in training neural networks is **matrix multiplication**—a mathematical process that involves multiplying matrices of numbers (data) together. Neural networks are essentially large-scale operations involving thousands or millions of these matrix multiplications.

The training process of neural networks involves adjusting the weights of these connections, a process that relies heavily on performing matrix multiplications repeatedly. This process is incredibly computationally intensive, particularly for deep networks with many layers of neurons. Matrix multiplications can be parallelized, making GPUs the perfect tool for handling these tasks efficiently.

The ability of GPUs to perform thousands of matrix multiplications in parallel drastically speeds up the training process. For example, in training a convolutional neural network (CNN) for image recognition, each image is passed through multiple layers of matrix transformations. These transformations are parallelized and processed at high speeds by GPUs, allowing for rapid training of models. The use of Tensor Cores only further accelerates this process, providing even more performance gains.

GPUs in Scientific Simulations and Research

In addition to their role in AI and machine learning, GPUs are also used extensively in **scientific simulations and research**. Fields such as physics, chemistry, biology, and climate modeling require vast amounts of computational power to simulate complex phenomena. GPUs have proven invaluable in these areas, as their ability to handle massive parallel workloads makes them ideal for processing the large datasets and performing the complex calculations required for simulations.

Scientific research often involves solving differential equations, simulating molecular structures, or modeling complex systems like weather patterns or fluid dynamics. These tasks involve significant amounts of data and require rapid calculations. GPUs can handle these operations far more efficiently than CPUs, accelerating research in fields ranging from climate science to drug discovery.

For example, in drug discovery, researchers use GPUs to simulate the interactions between molecules and predict their behavior in various environments. This allows scientists to test hypotheses much faster than traditional methods would permit, potentially speeding up the development of new medicines. Similarly, in physics, GPUs are used to simulate particle interactions or even the behavior of galaxies, providing insights that would otherwise take years to compute using traditional methods.

In computational fluid dynamics (CFD), GPUs are used to simulate the behavior of fluids in various conditions. Whether modeling airflow over an airplane wing or the movement of water in an ocean, GPUs accelerate simulations and provide more accurate results in less time. This is crucial for fields that require real-time simulations, such as engineering and environmental sciences.

The advent of GPUs has revolutionized scientific research by enabling researchers to tackle previously unsolvable problems, speeding up the discovery process, and enabling them to work with far larger datasets than ever before. The use of GPUs in these fields is not only changing the way we approach scientific problems but also pushing the boundaries of what we can achieve in fields ranging from artificial intelligence to quantum mechanics.

In conclusion, GPUs have expanded their role far beyond graphics rendering. They are now at the heart of the most groundbreaking advancements in AI, machine learning, and scientific research. Their unparalleled ability to perform parallel computations has allowed for faster, more efficient processing in a wide range of industries, paving the way for innovations that were once thought impossible. As GPU technology continues to evolve, its influence will only grow, driving further progress in fields ranging from healthcare to space exploration.

The Power of Parallel Processing

One of the key features that distinguishes a GPU from a CPU is its ability to perform **parallel processing**. While a CPU is optimized for sequential processing, handling one task at a time with high single-thread performance, a GPU is designed to handle multiple tasks simultaneously. This ability is at the core of why GPUs are so effective in processing complex computations, especially in applications like graphics rendering, scientific simulations, machine learning, and more.

To understand how GPUs achieve this massive parallelism, it's important to delve into the architecture that makes parallel execution possible. At the heart of a GPU is its design, which includes thousands of smaller, simpler cores that work in tandem to perform many operations at once. These cores are designed to handle large datasets and complex mathematical calculations, all while working simultaneously on different parts of the task at hand.

How GPUs Achieve Massive Parallelism

GPUs are engineered to excel at **Single Instruction, Multiple Data (SIMD)** processing, which allows them to perform the same operation across many data points simultaneously. This is in stark contrast to how CPUs operate, which typically execute instructions one after the other, focusing on a single task at a time.

To visualize how this works, consider a task like processing a large array of data. A CPU would process each data point sequentially, one by one. In contrast, a GPU can process many data points at once, with each core handling a different subset of the array simultaneously. This is what allows GPUs to handle tasks like graphics rendering and complex scientific calculations so much more efficiently than CPUs.

GPU Architecture: Thousands of Cores Working in Tandem

A typical modern GPU consists of **thousands of smaller cores** that are organized into groups called **Streaming Multiprocessors (SMs)**. Each of these cores is capable of performing calculations independently, yet they can also be synchronized to work together on larger tasks.

The GPU architecture is divided into **warps** (groups of 32 threads) that execute in lockstep. A single warp executes the same instruction across all its threads, making it highly efficient for parallel tasks. When a GPU is given a task, such as rendering a frame in a game, the work is broken down into thousands of small tasks. Each of these tasks is then distributed across the thousands of cores, and they all execute at the same time, speeding up the overall process.

The power of this parallel execution lies in the **granularity of the tasks** that GPUs perform. Unlike CPUs, which focus on general-purpose processing, GPUs excel at tasks that can be broken down into many smaller, identical pieces. This is why tasks like image processing, matrix multiplication, and physics simulations can be executed so efficiently on a GPU.

Key Concepts: Threads, Warps, and Blocks

To fully appreciate how GPUs achieve parallelism, it's important to understand how they organize their work. In GPU programming, the basic unit of execution is a **thread**. Each thread performs a small part of the task, such as processing a single pixel in an image or a single element in a matrix.

These threads are grouped into **blocks**, which are then grouped into **grids**. A grid can contain thousands or even millions of threads, with each block assigned to a different part of the task.

When a GPU executes a task, it sends the threads in a block to different cores. These threads run simultaneously, and since the GPU is capable of managing thousands of threads at once, the task is completed much faster than it would be if a CPU were used. This is a clear demonstration of the GPU's parallel processing power, which is its defining feature.

Warp Scheduling and Thread Execution

The GPU's execution model is designed for maximum parallel efficiency, but there are some nuances to how it schedules and executes threads. Threads within a warp are executed in lockstep, meaning that all threads in a warp execute the same instruction at the same time. This is referred to as **SIMT (Single Instruction, Multiple Threads)** execution.

However, not all threads in a warp may have data to process at any given time. When this happens, the GPU needs to handle **warp divergence**, which occurs when threads within the same warp take different execution paths (due to branching instructions, for example). While warp divergence can slow down processing because the GPU must wait for all threads to complete their work, modern GPUs are designed to handle this gracefully by re-scheduling threads as needed and minimizing the impact on performance.

The efficiency of GPU parallelism also depends on how well the workload can be divided among threads. Some tasks, like simple mathematical operations on large datasets, lend themselves well to parallel execution, while others may require more intricate management. Regardless, GPUs are built to handle tasks that involve a high degree of parallelism.

Benefits of Parallel Processing in Real-World Applications

The benefits of parallel processing extend far beyond the realm of gaming and graphics rendering. GPUs are increasingly being used for a wide range of computationally intensive tasks in industries such as **scientific research, financial modeling, artificial intelligence**, and even **cryptocurrency mining**.

In **artificial intelligence**, for example, deep learning models require the simultaneous processing of large amounts of data. The parallel processing capabilities of GPUs allow these models to be trained much faster than they would be on CPUs. This has accelerated the development of AI technologies, from voice recognition to autonomous vehicles, by allowing more complex models to be trained in less time.

In **scientific research**, GPUs are used to simulate complex physical systems, such as the behavior of molecules in chemistry or the movement of particles in physics. These simulations require immense computational power, and parallel processing allows them to be executed more quickly, enabling faster discoveries in fields like drug design, weather forecasting, and climate modeling.

Similarly, in **cryptocurrency mining**, GPUs are used to solve the complex mathematical problems required to validate transactions on blockchain networks. The high level of parallelism in GPU processing makes it well-suited for this task, enabling miners to perform the calculations much faster than with CPUs.

Conclusion

The power of parallel processing is what sets GPUs apart from traditional CPUs. With thousands of cores capable of executing many threads simultaneously, GPUs can handle massive datasets and perform complex calculations far more efficiently than a CPU ever could. This makes them indispensable in fields like graphics rendering, artificial intelligence, scientific simulations, and more. The ability to perform parallel processing on a massive scale is what allows GPUs to achieve the computational power required for the most demanding tasks in modern computing. As technology continues to advance, the role of parallel processing in GPUs will only grow, enabling even more groundbreaking innovations across industries.

Thread Blocks, Warps, and Streaming Multiprocessors

In a GPU, the architecture is designed to maximize efficiency by breaking down tasks into smaller chunks that can be processed in parallel. This breakdown involves organizing threads into **blocks**, which are further grouped into **warps** and managed by **Streaming Multiprocessors (SMs)**. Understanding these components and how they work together is key to appreciating the power of parallel processing in modern GPUs.

Thread Blocks

A **thread block** is the smallest unit of work that can be independently scheduled and executed by the GPU. Each block consists of a group of threads, typically in the range of 32 to several hundred, depending on the GPU's architecture. The threads within a block work in parallel, each executing the same instructions but on different pieces of data. These threads share resources like registers and shared memory, which allows them to work together efficiently on their assigned task.

Thread blocks are organized into a **grid**, which represents the entire task that the GPU is given. Each block is executed independently, and each thread within a block processes a different subset of data. Once all threads in a block have completed their work, the block finishes its execution, and the next block is scheduled for execution on the GPU cores.

Warps

Within each thread block, threads are grouped into **warps**. A warp is essentially a group of 32 threads that execute in lockstep, meaning that they all follow the same instruction at the same time. This design is crucial for maximizing parallelism in the GPU, as it ensures that many threads can be executed at once without requiring individual control over each one.

Warps are a critical part of the GPU's **SIMT (Single Instruction, Multiple Threads)** execution model. The entire warp of 32 threads runs the same instruction simultaneously, but each thread processes a different piece of data. For example, in a graphics rendering task, each thread might be responsible for processing a pixel on the screen, with the entire warp working on a small section of the image at once.

Because warps execute in lockstep, any **warp divergence**—when threads within a warp take different execution paths—can cause inefficiencies. The GPU must pause the execution of the warp while it handles the divergent paths, reducing performance. However, modern GPUs are designed to minimize this effect, allowing them to manage divergence and execute tasks as efficiently as possible.

Streaming Multiprocessors (SMs)

The **Streaming Multiprocessor (SM)** is the core processing unit in a GPU, and it plays a central role in managing thread blocks and warps. Each SM consists of multiple CUDA cores (or other processing units, depending on the architecture) and is responsible for executing the instructions of multiple warps at once. SMs are capable of handling several warps in parallel, which means that a GPU can process hundreds or even thousands of threads simultaneously.

In addition to the cores, SMs contain important hardware resources such as **shared memory**, **registers**, and **special function units**. Shared memory allows threads within the same block to communicate and share data efficiently, which is essential for optimizing performance. Registers store the data that threads operate on, and special function units handle complex operations like floating-point calculations and integer operations.

Each SM is designed to handle several warps at once, which means it can efficiently manage large-scale parallel tasks. This is a key reason why GPUs excel at workloads that require massive amounts of parallel computation, like graphics rendering, machine learning, and scientific simulations.

Optimizing Performance: Load Balancing and Data Sharing

For a GPU to perform at its best, managing load balancing and ensuring efficient data sharing between threads are crucial aspects. These strategies help maximize the throughput of the GPU and ensure that all of its resources are being utilized effectively.

Load Balancing

Load balancing refers to the process of ensuring that all thread blocks are assigned to SMs in such a way that no SM is overburdened while others are idle. Ideally, each SM should be handling an equal amount of work, and no thread block should be left waiting for resources or execution time.

The GPU scheduler is responsible for distributing thread blocks across available SMs. However, load balancing can be complex, especially when the workload is uneven or when some thread blocks require more resources than others. For instance, thread blocks that require more memory or more complex calculations may end up being scheduled to SMs that are already heavily loaded, leading to performance bottlenecks.

To avoid these issues, modern GPUs employ sophisticated load balancing algorithms that take into account the resources required by each thread block and ensure an even distribution of work. This helps prevent situations where some SMs are overworked while others remain underutilized, leading to optimal performance.

Data Sharing

Another key aspect of optimizing GPU performance is **data sharing** between threads. Since threads within the same block share resources like **shared memory**, they can communicate and share data more efficiently than threads in different blocks. This enables a higher level of cooperation between threads, which is essential for tasks like matrix multiplication, image processing, and simulations that involve large datasets.

Efficient use of shared memory is critical to achieving high performance on GPUs. Shared memory is much faster than global memory (the memory accessible to all threads on the GPU), but it is also limited in size. Therefore, optimizing data sharing involves ensuring that threads use shared memory for frequently accessed data, while minimizing access to global memory to reduce latency and improve throughput.

In addition to shared memory, thread synchronization is also an important consideration for data sharing. Threads within a block may need to wait for others to finish their computations before they can proceed. To manage this, GPUs use **barrier synchronization** mechanisms, which ensure that all threads within a block reach a certain point before continuing. This helps ensure that threads are not working with incomplete or outdated data, which could lead to incorrect results.

The Importance of Memory Hierarchy

The memory hierarchy within a GPU is another key factor in optimizing performance. GPUs use multiple levels of memory, each with its own speed and size characteristics. These include **global memory**, **shared memory**, **local memory**, and **registers**. Each of these memory types has its own advantages and trade-offs, and efficient memory management is essential for ensuring that the GPU can perform as efficiently as possible.

For example, **registers** are the fastest form of memory and are used to store data that is frequently accessed by threads. However, they are limited in size, so managing how and when data is stored in registers is an important consideration. **Shared memory** is faster than global memory but limited in size, and it must be used wisely to maximize its effectiveness.

By understanding how data flows through the GPU's memory hierarchy and ensuring that threads use the most appropriate memory type for their data, developers can further optimize the performance of GPU-based applications.

Conclusion

The architecture of GPUs, with its thread blocks, warps, and streaming multiprocessors, is designed for maximum parallel efficiency. By organizing work into small tasks that can be executed simultaneously, GPUs are able to achieve incredible levels of computational power. Optimizing performance on a GPU involves ensuring that load balancing is handled correctly and that data sharing between threads is efficient. Through careful management of these resources, GPUs can handle some of the most demanding tasks in modern computing, from graphics rendering to machine learning and scientific simulations. Understanding these concepts is crucial for anyone looking to harness the full potential of GPU technology.

Chapter 7: Modern GPU Technologies and Trends

Ray Tracing Cores and Real-Time Ray Tracing

As technology advances, GPUs continue to push the boundaries of graphical fidelity, with **ray tracing** standing out as one of the most groundbreaking developments in recent years. Ray tracing is a rendering technique that simulates the way light interacts with objects in a scene to produce highly realistic lighting, reflections, and shadows. Traditionally, ray tracing has been too computationally expensive for real-time applications like video games and interactive media, but with the advent of **ray tracing cores** in modern GPUs, real-time ray tracing has become a reality.

Ray Tracing Cores: The Heart of Real-Time Ray Tracing

Ray tracing cores are specialized hardware units embedded within modern GPUs, designed specifically to accelerate ray tracing calculations. These cores are optimized to trace the path of light as it interacts with objects in a 3D environment, calculating how light bounces off surfaces, refracts through materials, and casts realistic shadows. By offloading this computationally intense process to dedicated hardware, ray tracing cores enable real-time rendering of complex lighting effects that were previously impossible to achieve in video games and interactive applications.

The introduction of **NVIDIA's RTX series**, featuring dedicated **RT cores** (Ray Tracing Cores), revolutionized real-time ray tracing. These cores allow for the simultaneous calculation of many rays of light, enhancing visual realism by simulating effects such as global illumination, reflections, and refractions in real-time. The result is a more immersive experience with lighting that reacts to the environment in a way that closely mirrors how it behaves in the real world.

For example, in a video game, ray tracing can produce lifelike reflections on surfaces, such as a mirror-like pond or glass, showing an accurate reflection of the scene that responds dynamically to player movements. This level of realism, once thought to be reserved for pre-rendered scenes, has now entered the world of interactive graphics, significantly raising the bar for visual fidelity.

Real-Time Ray Tracing in Gaming and Beyond

Real-time ray tracing has not only redefined the gaming experience but is also having a profound impact on industries such as film production, architectural visualization, and virtual simulations. In gaming, developers have started to implement ray tracing effects in many AAA titles, providing players with a more immersive and visually stunning experience. Games like **Control**, **Cyberpunk 2077**, and **Minecraft** have integrated ray tracing to provide breathtaking visuals, where lighting, shadows, and reflections contribute to a more lifelike and engaging environment.

Beyond gaming, ray tracing is becoming an essential tool for professionals in fields like visual effects and computer-aided design (CAD). Artists and designers can now render photorealistic scenes in real-time, enabling faster iteration and more efficient workflows. For instance, in architectural design, real-time ray tracing allows designers to visualize how natural light will interact with their structures throughout the day, making it easier to optimize building aesthetics and energy efficiency.

As GPU manufacturers continue to refine their ray tracing technology, the fidelity of real-time ray tracing is expected to improve, bringing even more realistic lighting effects and visual enhancements to gaming and beyond.

Advances in Cooling and Power Efficiency

As GPUs become increasingly powerful, managing heat and power consumption has become a critical challenge for manufacturers. With the rising computational demands of modern GPUs, the need for advanced **cooling** systems and **power-efficient** designs has never been more apparent. GPUs are responsible for rendering highly complex images, performing computations for artificial intelligence (AI), and running data-heavy simulations, all of which generate significant heat. Without proper cooling, the performance of GPUs could degrade, or worse, they could become damaged.

Cooling Solutions: Keeping GPUs Running at Peak Performance

To address the issue of heat generation, GPU manufacturers have developed increasingly sophisticated cooling solutions. Traditional cooling methods, such as air cooling with fans, have been supplemented or replaced by advanced technologies designed to handle the immense heat output of modern GPUs.

One of the most popular cooling innovations is **liquid cooling**, which uses liquid-filled tubes and a radiator to draw heat away from the GPU. Liquid cooling systems are highly efficient and can handle the high thermal loads generated by top-tier GPUs, allowing them to maintain stable performance even under heavy loads. These systems can be found in high-performance gaming PCs and workstations, where users demand optimal performance for extended periods.

For users who prefer simpler setups, **hybrid cooling** solutions are also available. These combine the best of air and liquid cooling, with a liquid cooler used in conjunction with strategically placed fans to maximize heat dissipation. Hybrid systems are less complex than fully liquid-cooled setups but still provide excellent thermal management.

Manufacturers are also focusing on the **thermal design** of the GPU itself. For example, new GPUs come with larger heat sinks and more advanced materials, such as **graphene**, which offer better thermal conductivity than traditional copper. These materials are integrated into the GPU's design to help dissipate heat more efficiently and maintain a safe operating temperature.

Power Efficiency: Maximizing Performance While Minimizing Power Consumption

As GPUs become more powerful, they require more power to fuel their increased computational capabilities. However, power consumption has always been a concern, especially for mobile devices, laptops, and gaming consoles, where battery life and thermal limitations come into play. To combat this, GPU manufacturers have invested heavily in improving the **power efficiency** of their designs, ensuring that GPUs can deliver high performance without consuming excessive amounts of electricity.

Modern GPUs employ several strategies to optimize power consumption. One of the most effective is **dynamic voltage and frequency scaling** (DVFS), which allows the GPU to adjust its power usage based on the workload. When the GPU is performing less demanding tasks, such as idle periods or light workloads, it reduces its power consumption by lowering its clock speed and voltage. On the other hand, during heavy workloads, such as gaming or complex computations, the GPU can ramp up its performance by increasing its power consumption. This dynamic approach ensures that power is only used when necessary, improving overall efficiency.

Another important advancement is the development of **power management chips** that work in tandem with the GPU to monitor and regulate power usage. These chips help ensure that the GPU operates within safe power limits, preventing overheating and ensuring long-term reliability.

NVIDIA's Ampere architecture, for instance, features improvements in power efficiency, allowing GPUs to achieve better performance-per-watt. This means that the GPUs can deliver higher performance while using less power, which is essential for both desktop and mobile devices. Power efficiency is becoming even more critical with the increasing popularity of mobile gaming and laptop GPUs, where long battery life and thermal constraints are paramount.

The Future of Cooling and Power Efficiency

As GPUs continue to advance, cooling and power efficiency will remain at the forefront of design considerations. Future GPUs will likely employ even more advanced materials and cooling technologies, such as **phase change cooling** or **micro-channel cooling**, which can improve thermal dissipation without adding bulk. Additionally, with the rise of **AI-driven**

workloads and **cloud gaming**, there will be a growing emphasis on creating GPUs that can deliver high performance while maintaining low power consumption to reduce environmental impact and improve system sustainability.

With more powerful GPUs driving the future of gaming, AI, and data science, manufacturers will continue to innovate and refine cooling and power management solutions to ensure that these systems can meet the demands of modern applications without sacrificing efficiency or performance.

Ray tracing cores and real-time ray tracing have revolutionized the way graphics are rendered, offering unprecedented visual realism in gaming and professional applications alike. Meanwhile, advances in cooling and power efficiency are ensuring that GPUs can handle the ever-increasing computational demands without compromising performance or reliability. As these technologies evolve, GPUs will continue to push the boundaries of what's possible in visual fidelity, AI processing, and beyond, shaping the future of computing in profound ways.

GPUs for Virtual Reality (VR) and Augmented Reality (AR)

As we step into an era of immersive digital experiences, GPUs have become the backbone of cutting-edge technologies like **Virtual Reality (VR)** and **Augmented Reality (AR)**. These technologies rely on the processing power of GPUs to create lifelike environments and seamless interactions that blur the lines between the physical and digital worlds.

The Role of GPUs in VR and AR

In both VR and AR, **real-time rendering** is key to creating immersive experiences. GPUs are responsible for generating the high-quality images and video that are essential for these experiences. Unlike traditional gaming, where you view a screen from a fixed position, VR requires the GPU to render the entire environment in real-time from multiple angles, updating the scene at an extremely high frame rate (often 90 frames per second or higher) to maintain a smooth experience and avoid motion sickness.

VR, in particular, demands high processing power because it involves creating fully immersive, 3D environments where every object and every action must respond to the user's movements in real-time. The GPU's ability to render complex 3D models and textures, coupled with ultra-low latency, is critical to achieving a realistic and comfortable VR experience. Graphics cards must manage high-resolution rendering for each eye (typically 4K or higher), creating a stereoscopic effect that enhances depth perception and realism.

AR, on the other hand, overlays digital information onto the real world, requiring the GPU to process both the environment around the user and the digital elements that are placed within that environment. While not as demanding as VR in terms of immersion, AR requires the GPU to handle multiple data streams at once, such as live video feeds, environmental mapping, and interactive 3D objects. The GPU's ability to seamlessly integrate virtual objects into the real world, ensuring that they stay fixed in place as the user moves, is essential to creating a convincing AR experience.

Both VR and AR require GPUs to perform rapid calculations and maintain high performance while also minimizing latency. Even small delays or stuttering in the graphics can cause discomfort or disrupt the sense of immersion, making high-quality GPUs a fundamental component in the success of these technologies.

Challenges and Considerations in VR and AR

While GPUs are critical to the success of VR and AR, there are several challenges that must be addressed to enhance these experiences:

- **Latency:** One of the primary concerns in VR and AR is latency, the time it takes for a GPU to render an image after receiving input from the user. High latency can cause nausea and motion sickness, disrupting the immersion and making the experience uncomfortable. Low-latency GPUs are essential to smooth, comfortable VR and AR applications.
- **Frame Rate and Resolution:** For a truly immersive experience, VR and AR applications require high frame rates and resolutions. Any dips in frame rate can result in motion blur or stuttering, both of which are detrimental to the overall experience. GPUs must maintain consistent high performance to render the content smoothly.
- **Thermal Management:** VR and AR applications are highly demanding, often pushing the GPU to its limits for extended periods. Effective cooling solutions are required to prevent the GPU from overheating during intense sessions.

The continuous development of specialized GPU architectures is addressing these challenges, and **NVIDIA's VR-ready GPUs** and **AMD's RDNA architecture** are prime examples of GPUs designed specifically to enhance VR and AR performance. As VR and AR hardware advances, it is expected that GPUs will evolve to meet even more stringent requirements for performance, realism, and interaction.

Future Trends in GPU Development

The GPU landscape is constantly evolving, driven by advancements in technology and the increasing demand for higher performance in both consumer and professional applications. As we look to the future, several key trends are emerging that will shape the next generation of GPUs.

AI and Machine Learning Integration

One of the most exciting trends in GPU development is the increasing integration of **artificial intelligence (AI)** and **machine learning (ML)** capabilities. Modern GPUs are already essential for training and running AI models, and this trend is expected to accelerate as AI becomes more prevalent in fields like healthcare, autonomous vehicles, and robotics.

Next-generation GPUs will likely feature even more specialized cores and processing units dedicated to AI tasks. These units will be optimized for matrix multiplications, neural network training, and inference, allowing AI applications to run more efficiently and at larger scales. GPUs designed for AI and ML will also benefit from **Tensor Cores** (specialized hardware for AI processing), as seen in NVIDIA's **Volta** and **Ampere** architectures, which are already accelerating workloads in deep learning.

Quantum Computing and GPUs

Though still in its infancy, **quantum computing** represents a major frontier in computational power, and GPUs will likely play a role in the development of this next-generation technology. Quantum computing promises to solve complex problems far beyond the capabilities of traditional classical computers by using quantum bits (qubits) instead of binary bits. GPUs will be instrumental in simulating quantum algorithms and performing other tasks related to quantum computing, helping researchers and developers navigate the complexities of this emerging field.

Next-Generation Rendering: Path Tracing and Beyond

As GPU technology advances, rendering techniques will become increasingly sophisticated. The next frontier in graphics rendering is **path tracing**, an advanced form of ray tracing that simulates how light interacts with every surface in a scene, accounting for reflections, refractions, and light scattering in a highly accurate manner. Unlike traditional ray tracing, which traces rays of light in a direct path, path tracing follows multiple paths of light for more realistic results, though at a significantly higher computational cost.

While path tracing will be a significant challenge for GPUs, future generations of GPUs will likely be optimized to handle this intensive process. The goal will be to deliver even higher levels of realism in real-time applications, pushing the limits of photorealistic rendering in games, simulations, and virtual worlds.

Enhanced Power Efficiency and Sustainability

With growing concerns about the environmental impact of technology, **power efficiency** will continue to be a major focus for GPU development. Modern GPUs are already quite efficient, but as they become more powerful, manufacturers will need to design them to consume less power without sacrificing performance. This trend will be especially important in mobile devices, laptops, and other energy-conscious applications.

In addition to energy efficiency, the use of **sustainable materials** in GPU manufacturing will become a priority. With an increased global focus on sustainability, GPU manufacturers will likely prioritize eco-friendly production methods, recycling, and minimizing the environmental impact of their products.

Integration with Cloud Computing and Edge Computing

The increasing shift toward **cloud computing** and **edge computing** will also drive GPU innovation. As computing tasks move away from local devices and onto cloud-based platforms, GPUs will play a crucial role in providing the processing power needed for everything from gaming and video rendering to AI-driven workloads.

Cloud-based gaming services, such as **NVIDIA's GeForce NOW** and **Google Stadia**, already rely on powerful GPUs in data centers to deliver high-quality gaming experiences to users without the need for a high-end gaming PC. As cloud services grow, the demand for GPU power in the cloud will only increase, pushing manufacturers to create more powerful and scalable solutions for the cloud.

On the edge computing front, GPUs will be essential for processing data closer to the source, such as in autonomous vehicles, IoT devices, and industrial applications. GPUs in edge devices will need to balance power efficiency and computational performance, handling complex tasks like object detection, video analysis, and real-time decision-making.

The Rise of Custom GPUs and Personalized Solutions

Finally, **custom GPUs** are expected to become more prevalent as different industries require tailored solutions for specific tasks. For example, the use of custom GPUs for AI research, cryptocurrency mining, and gaming is on the rise, with companies designing specialized GPUs to meet the unique demands of these fields. Custom GPUs could also be optimized for use in specific devices, such as smartphones, VR headsets, and embedded systems, ensuring the perfect balance of power and efficiency.

As technology continues to evolve, GPUs will remain at the heart of the next generation of digital experiences, from AI-driven advancements to immersive virtual worlds. The future of GPU technology is bound to bring even more innovations that will shape the way we interact with the digital world.

Chapter 8: Challenges in GPU Design and Manufacturing

Heat Dissipation and Cooling

One of the most pressing challenges in GPU design and manufacturing is **heat dissipation**. As GPUs become more powerful, they generate more heat during operation. This is especially true for high-performance GPUs used in gaming, machine learning, cryptocurrency mining, and other demanding applications. Efficient cooling systems are critical for maintaining stable performance, preventing thermal throttling, and prolonging the lifespan of the GPU.

The Physics of Heat Generation

At the heart of the issue is the sheer density of processing power in modern GPUs. GPUs contain millions of transistors that process vast amounts of data in parallel, which naturally generates heat as a byproduct of electrical resistance. The more calculations a GPU performs, the more heat it generates, and this heat must be dissipated effectively to prevent damage to the hardware.

The amount of heat produced by high-end GPUs is substantial. High-performance cards, especially those designed for 4K gaming or AI workloads, can reach temperatures of 80-90°C (176-194°F) under heavy load, which is far too high for components to function efficiently or safely without cooling.

Cooling Solutions: Air vs. Liquid

To manage heat, manufacturers have developed various cooling methods, and these methods can generally be divided into two categories: **air cooling** and **liquid cooling**.

- **Air Cooling:** This is the most common and cost-effective cooling solution for consumer GPUs. Air cooling typically involves a combination of **heat sinks** and **fans**. The heat sink absorbs heat from the GPU and dissipates it into the surrounding air, while the fan helps to expel the hot air and draw in cooler air. High-performance air cooling systems use multiple fans and advanced heat sinks made of materials like **copper** or **aluminum** to optimize heat transfer.
- **Liquid Cooling:** For top-tier GPUs, especially in workstations or gaming PCs where heat generation is at its highest, **liquid cooling** systems are becoming more

common. These systems involve a liquid coolant that circulates around the GPU, carrying heat away from the core and releasing it via a radiator. Liquid cooling is much more efficient than air cooling and is capable of handling the high thermal demands of next-gen GPUs. Some high-end gaming systems even integrate full **liquid cooling loops**, which cool both the CPU and GPU for maximum thermal performance.

While liquid cooling offers superior thermal management, it comes at a higher cost and complexity. Additionally, liquid cooling systems are more prone to failure, particularly with leaks or pump malfunctions, which can damage components.

Thermal Throttling: A Necessary Evil

Despite advanced cooling solutions, **thermal throttling** remains a reality. Throttling occurs when the GPU detects excessive heat and automatically reduces its performance to prevent overheating and damage. While this is a protective measure, it can negatively impact performance, especially during demanding tasks like gaming or machine learning.

Manufacturers are constantly working on innovative designs and materials to mitigate thermal throttling and increase the overall heat dissipation efficiency. For example, **graphene-based thermal interfaces** are being explored for their superior heat conductivity properties, which could help in more effective cooling without adding significant weight or bulk.

Memory Bandwidth and Latency Issues

Another critical challenge in GPU design lies in addressing the balance between **memory bandwidth** and **latency**. As GPUs become more powerful, they require more memory and faster access to that memory to handle the increasing complexity of modern tasks, whether it's rendering a 3D scene or processing large AI datasets.

Memory Bandwidth

Memory bandwidth refers to the rate at which data can be read from or written to the GPU's memory. Higher memory bandwidth allows the GPU to access more data faster, which is particularly important when dealing with high-resolution textures, large models, or large datasets. However, memory bandwidth is often a bottleneck in GPU performance, as it can only go as fast as the memory can handle.

For example, **HBM2** (High Bandwidth Memory 2), which is used in some high-end GPUs, offers significantly higher bandwidth than traditional **GDDR** (Graphics Double Data Rate) memory, but it's also more expensive to implement. This creates a challenge for GPU manufacturers, who must balance performance and cost when selecting the type of memory to use in their designs.

As the complexity of workloads increases, GPUs demand higher memory bandwidth to avoid bottlenecks. Insufficient bandwidth can lead to slower rendering times, lag, or stuttering in demanding applications like 4K gaming or machine learning.

Memory Latency

Memory latency is the time it takes for the GPU to access a specific piece of data in memory. The lower the latency, the faster the GPU can retrieve data and perform calculations. In general, GPUs need to have both high bandwidth and low latency to deliver optimal performance.

Reducing memory latency can be particularly challenging in GPUs because of the sheer volume of data they process. As GPUs continue to push the envelope of computational power, memory latency becomes a more significant challenge. To reduce latency, manufacturers are developing new memory architectures and employing techniques like **cache memory** to store frequently accessed data closer to the GPU cores, reducing the need to fetch it from main memory.

The Impact on Performance

Both memory bandwidth and latency have a direct impact on GPU performance. For instance, **high latency** can cause data to be delayed before it can be processed, which can slow down the overall rendering process. Similarly, insufficient memory bandwidth can cause the GPU to wait for data, leading to delays in processing tasks and a reduction in overall performance.

To address these issues, manufacturers are incorporating more **memory channels** and **larger memory pools** to ensure that data can be accessed quickly. Memory bandwidth is often increased by using faster memory types or multiple memory modules. Meanwhile, **advanced memory architectures** like **NVIDIA's NVLink** and **AMD's Infinity Fabric**are being developed to provide a more efficient, high-bandwidth connection between the GPU and its memory, allowing for faster data access and higher overall throughput.

Future Innovations

As GPUs continue to evolve, there will be continued advancements in memory technology to meet the ever-growing demands of high-end computing tasks. Some potential future developments include:

- **High Bandwidth Memory 3 (HBM3):** Expected to deliver even greater bandwidth than HBM2, providing better performance for next-generation GPUs.
- **Increased Use of On-chip Memory:** Rather than relying entirely on off-chip memory, GPUs may incorporate more **on-chip memory** that can be accessed at incredibly high speeds.
- **Faster Interconnects:** With more advanced interconnect technologies, GPUs will be able to communicate with memory and other components more efficiently, further reducing latency.

In conclusion, the challenges associated with **heat dissipation**, **memory bandwidth**, and **latency** are ongoing hurdles in the design and manufacturing of GPUs. As GPU performance continues to improve, these challenges will become more complex, requiring innovative solutions and the development of new technologies. The future of GPU design will be defined by the balance between performance, efficiency, and cost, with manufacturers continually pushing the boundaries of what's possible in high-performance computing.

As GPUs become more powerful, one of the most significant trade-offs developers and engineers face is the **balance between energy consumption** and **performance**. GPUs, especially high-end models used in gaming, machine learning, scientific simulations, and cryptocurrency mining, demand substantial amounts of power to achieve the computational performance required for these tasks. The more powerful the GPU, the more energy it consumes, which raises important questions about sustainability, operational costs, and environmental impact.

The Power Demands of High-End GPUs

Modern GPUs, particularly those designed for **gaming** or **data center workloads**, can consume anywhere from **200 watts** to over **400 watts** of power during peak usage, with some even pushing well over 500 watts. This is a significant increase compared to earlier generations of GPUs, which were less power-hungry. While the performance gains are undeniable, the power required to achieve these gains presents challenges both for individual consumers and large-scale operations like data centers.

For example, when you consider GPUs in **cloud computing** or **machine learning** environments, the need for numerous high-performance GPUs running continuously leads to a substantial increase in energy consumption. The rise of AI models like GPT (the model you're interacting with) and deep learning applications often requires thousands of GPUs running in parallel for extended periods, significantly adding to the overall energy demand.

The Heat-Performance Trade-Off

The amount of energy a GPU uses is directly correlated to the heat it generates, and managing this heat becomes even more critical as energy consumption increases. Companies are continuously working to develop more energy-efficient GPUs that provide **maximum performance** while **minimizing power usage**.

For example, **NVIDIA's Ampere architecture** and **AMD's RDNA 2 architecture** offer performance improvements over previous generations while implementing power efficiency technologies. These architectures feature **dynamic voltage and frequency scaling** (DVFS) and **power gating** to optimize power use during periods of low workload, reducing power consumption when the GPU is not under heavy load.

Another key strategy to improve energy efficiency without sacrificing performance is the development of **multi-chip modules (MCM)**. This approach involves using several smaller, power-efficient chips that work together to perform the same task, thus balancing the power demand between multiple components and improving efficiency.

The Environmental Impact

Energy consumption also brings with it an environmental concern. The more power GPUs require, the greater the carbon footprint associated with their use. Data centers, which use large clusters of GPUs to handle everything from web hosting to machine learning workloads, are some of the largest consumers of energy worldwide. As climate change and sustainability become more pressing global issues, reducing the environmental impact of technology, including GPUs, will become an increasing priority for manufacturers and consumers alike.

In response to this, many companies are investing in **green energy solutions** such as renewable energy sources, including wind and solar power, to offset the environmental impact of their operations. Some GPU manufacturers are also focusing on more sustainable manufacturing practices, including the use of **recycled materials** and reducing the energy intensity of production processes.

Supply Chain and Scalability Challenges

In addition to the challenges posed by energy consumption, **GPU manufacturers** face several other obstacles when it comes to scaling production and maintaining efficient supply chains. These challenges, which are felt most acutely during periods of high demand, have profound implications for both the cost and availability of GPUs.

Semiconductor Shortages

One of the primary factors influencing GPU availability and cost is the global **semiconductor shortage**. Semiconductors are critical components of GPUs, and supply chain disruptions in semiconductor manufacturing have caused a significant delay in production timelines. This shortage, which has persisted for several years, has led to a mismatch between supply and demand, resulting in higher prices for consumers and difficulties in acquiring GPUs for high-performance computing tasks.

Manufacturers are working hard to address this issue by investing in new production facilities and scaling up their operations. However, building new semiconductor plants is a lengthy and costly process, often taking years to complete. Additionally, the complex supply chain that stretches across multiple countries, from **raw material extraction** to **final assembly**, is vulnerable to disruptions from factors like geopolitical tensions, pandemics, or natural disasters.

Scalability Challenges for Data Centers

For data centers and large-scale operations, **scalability** is another challenge when it comes to deploying GPUs. The ability to scale GPU usage efficiently and cost-effectively is essential for businesses that rely on these powerful processing units for tasks like machine learning or rendering large-scale simulations.

One of the main issues in scaling GPU deployment is the **cost and logistics** involved in adding additional hardware to a data center. With GPUs consuming significant power and generating substantial heat, scaling requires more sophisticated infrastructure. This includes additional **power supplies**, **cooling solutions**, and **networking capabilities** to handle the increased workload. Additionally, **space limitations** in data centers may constrain the number of GPUs that can be physically deployed.

Manufacturing Lead Times and Demand Fluctuations

The demand for GPUs is often cyclical, with peaks in demand driven by major product launches, gaming trends, or external events like cryptocurrency mining booms. However, manufacturing lead times are long, which means that there can be significant delays between the moment a new product is announced and when it becomes widely available.

This can create periods of high demand and low supply, driving up prices and making it difficult for consumers to purchase GPUs at reasonable prices.

In particular, **new-generation GPUs** often see inflated prices during their launch periods due to limited availability. Manufacturers, meanwhile, are often forced to prioritize large orders from major corporations or cloud service providers, leaving individual consumers with fewer options.

The Need for More Efficient Manufacturing

To overcome these challenges, manufacturers are looking for ways to streamline production and make the supply chain more resilient. This includes investing in **automated manufacturing systems** to increase throughput and reduce reliance on human labor. Additionally, **3D stacking** and **chiplet-based designs** are being explored as potential solutions to increase the efficiency of GPU production.

As technology continues to evolve, manufacturers will need to adopt more **flexible** and **scalable production processes** to meet the growing demand for GPUs while mitigating the risks of supply chain disruptions. The rise of **cloud gaming** and **AI-powered applications** is expected to drive further demand, making these scalability challenges even more critical.

Geopolitical and Trade Risks

Beyond the technological and logistical challenges, GPU manufacturers must also contend with **geopolitical risks**. As the world's largest semiconductor producers are concentrated in a few regions, particularly **East Asia** and the **United States**, political tensions and trade wars between these countries can create significant disruptions in the supply of raw materials, parts, or finished products.

For example, trade restrictions on critical materials like **rare earth metals** or components like **graphics chips** could delay production and increase costs. The rise of **protectionist policies** in some countries can further complicate the smooth flow of goods in the global GPU supply chain.

Conclusion

The challenges of **energy consumption** and **supply chain scalability** are central to the future of GPU technology. As GPUs continue to push the boundaries of performance and power, manufacturers must find ways to balance these demands with environmental concerns, efficiency, and cost. The ongoing semiconductor shortages, demand fluctuations, and geopolitical risks add further complexity to the landscape, highlighting the need for **innovative solutions** in both manufacturing and resource management. The next chapter of GPU evolution will depend not only on improving raw performance but also on creating a more sustainable and scalable ecosystem to support the increasingly power-hungry world of modern computing

Chapter 9: Choosing the Right Graphics Card

Selecting the right graphics card can feel like a daunting task, especially given the myriad of options available in the market today. Whether you're a gamer, a professional working in content creation, or someone interested in machine learning, choosing a GPU that aligns with your needs, budget, and goals is crucial. In this chapter, we'll break down the key factors to consider when choosing a graphics card and explore some of the most popular GPU brands and models available on the market today.

Factors to Consider

1. Performance Needs

The first and most important factor to consider when choosing a GPU is the level of performance you require. cards are designed for different use cases, and the performance you need will vary based on your primary activities.

- **For Gaming**: Gamers often seek the highest possible frame rates, smooth gameplay, and high-quality visuals. If you're a gamer, you'll want a GPU that can handle the latest games at the highest settings. Look for GPUs with higher clock speeds, more CUDA cores, and ample VRAM to ensure seamless gameplay at resolutions like 1080p, 1440p, and 4K.

- **For Content Creation and Video Editing**: If you're a creator who works with 3D rendering, video editing, or animation, you'll need a GPU with strong computational power. GPUs with larger memory bandwidth and more VRAM are essential for handling complex tasks, rendering large video files, and working with large datasets in applications like Adobe Premiere Pro or Blender.
- **For Machine Learning and AI**: In machine learning, GPUs are crucial for training models efficiently. The performance you need will depend on the complexity of the models you're working with. GPUs with tensor cores (like NVIDIA's A100 or Tesla series) are designed specifically for AI workloads, providing high throughput for matrix multiplications and neural network computations.

2. Budget

Price is often the deciding factor for many when selecting a graphics card. High-end GPUs from brands like NVIDIA and AMD can cost several hundred or even thousands of dollars, while more budget-friendly options offer adequate performance for general tasks or entry-level gaming.

Here's a breakdown of GPU options at different price points:

- **Entry-Level GPUs**: Suitable for casual gaming and basic tasks like web browsing and light photo editing. These GPUs often range from **$100 to $200** and offer good performance for older games and lower graphical settings.
- **Mid-Range GPUs**: These are the go-to choice for most gamers, offering solid performance for modern games at 1080p and 1440p resolutions. Prices typically range from **$250 to $500**.
- **High-End GPUs**: High-performance GPUs for 4K gaming, video editing, or AI workloads. These can cost **$600 and up**, with premium models like NVIDIA's RTX 3080, RTX 3090, or AMD's RX 6900 XT reaching well over **$1,000**.
- **Professional GPUs**: If you're working in content creation, scientific computing, or deep learning, professional GPUs like NVIDIA's **Quadro** series or AMD's **Radeon Pro** series may be worth the investment.

These cards are priced similarly to high-end consumer models but often come with specialized features, such as certified drivers for professional applications.

3. Use Case

Your specific use case will also influence the graphics card you choose. While gaming and content creation are two of the most common use cases, other professional needs such as **CAD** (computer-aided design), **virtualization**, or **cryptocurrency mining** can also dictate the specifications of your GPU.

- **Gaming**: Choose a GPU with high frame rates and a robust cooling solution for extended gaming sessions. Opt for a card that supports **ray tracing** for the latest graphical enhancements and high-quality visual effects.
- **Professional Work (Video Editing, CAD, 3D Rendering)**: A higher-end GPU with more VRAM is crucial for editing high-resolution videos, working with large models, or rendering 3D content. GPUs with **hardware-accelerated encoding/decoding** (such as NVIDIA's

NVENC) can also make the editing process more efficient.

- **Cryptocurrency Mining**: For mining cryptocurrencies like Ethereum, choose a GPU that provides a good balance between performance and power efficiency. Popular models for mining include NVIDIA's **RTX 30-series** and AMD's **RX 6000 series**.

Popular GPU Brands and Models

Several manufacturers produce graphics cards, with **NVIDIA** and **AMD** being the most prominent. Both companies offer a range of GPUs that cater to different user needs, from entry-level to high-end professionals.

NVIDIA

NVIDIA is a market leader, particularly known for its **GeForce** and **Quadro** series, which dominate the gaming and professional sectors, respectively.

- **GeForce RTX 30 Series (Ampere Architecture)**:
    - **RTX 3090**: Targeted at enthusiasts, this card provides unparalleled gaming performance, ideal for 4K and 8K gaming, with a massive 24GB of VRAM.

- **RTX 3080**: Offers excellent 4K gaming performance at a more affordable price point than the 3090, with 10GB of VRAM.
- **RTX 3070**: A high-performance option for gamers aiming for 1440p or 4K gaming, with 8GB of VRAM.
- **RTX 3060 Ti/3060**: Budget-friendly options for 1080p and 1440p gaming, offering great value for money at lower prices.
- **Quadro Series (Professional GPUs)**:
  - **Quadro RTX 8000**: A professional-grade GPU for workstations that excels in deep learning, 3D rendering, and scientific simulations with 48GB of VRAM.
  - **Quadro P2000**: A mid-range professional GPU for CAD, content creation, and visualization with 5GB of VRAM.
- **Tesla Series (Data Center GPUs)**:
  - **NVIDIA A100**: Targeted at AI researchers and data scientists, offering incredible performance in machine learning tasks, with a focus on deep learning workloads.

AMD

AMD has made substantial strides in recent years, particularly with its **Radeon RX** and **Radeon Pro** series. While AMD GPUs are often seen as offering better price-to-performance ratios, they are also known for offering excellent gaming performance, especially in the mid-range market.

- **Radeon RX 6000 Series**:
    - **RX 6900 XT**: AMD's flagship gaming GPU, competing with NVIDIA's RTX 3090, offering excellent 4K gaming performance.
    - **RX 6800 XT**: A high-performance GPU with 16GB of GDDR6 VRAM, offering great value for gamers looking to hit 1440p or 4K.
    - **RX 6700 XT**: A mid-range offering aimed at 1440p gaming, with 12GB of VRAM, providing great performance at a more accessible price.
    - **RX 6600 XT**: A budget-friendly option for 1080p gaming with solid performance for entry-level gamers.
- **Radeon Pro Series** (Professional GPUs):
    - **Radeon Pro VII**: Targeted at professional content creators and engineers, providing strong performance for 3D modeling and video rendering tasks.

- ○ **Radeon Pro W5700**: Designed for mid-range professional workstations, supporting CAD, content creation, and VR development.

Other Notable Brands

- **EVGA**: Known for its premium-quality NVIDIA-based graphics cards, EVGA offers high-end models with superior cooling and factory overclocking for better performance.
- **MSI**: Produces both NVIDIA and AMD GPUs, with a focus on reliability, build quality, and innovative cooling solutions.
- **Asus**: Known for its **ROG Strix** and **TUF Gaming** series, offering top-tier graphics cards with strong performance and durability.
- **Gigabyte**: Offers a range of gaming and professional-grade graphics cards with innovative cooling systems and factory overclocked models.

Conclusion

When choosing a graphics card, there are several factors to consider, including performance requirements, budget, and your specific use case. Whether you're a gamer, content creator, or AI enthusiast, there's a GPU that suits your needs.

NVIDIA and AMD offer an extensive range of GPUs that cater to all performance levels and price points, and other brands like EVGA, MSI, and Asus provide high-quality alternatives with premium features.

By understanding your requirements and the specifications of various GPU models, you'll be able to make an informed decision that will offer the best performance for your needs without breaking the bank.

Gaming vs. Professional GPUs

When choosing between gaming and professional GPUs, the decision largely depends on the intended use and performance needs of the user. While gaming GPUs and professional GPUs share similar core technologies, their optimization and feature sets vary to cater to different industries and workloads. In this section, we will explore the differences between gaming and professional GPUs and how to choose the right one based on your specific requirements.

Gaming GPUs

Gaming GPUs are designed primarily for rendering high-quality graphics in video games, offering high frame rates, vivid textures, and realistic lighting.

These GPUs prioritize performance in environments that demand fast rendering, responsiveness, and visual fidelity. Gaming GPUs are optimized to handle games at various resolutions (1080p, 1440p, 4K) and provide smooth, immersive experiences.

- **Performance Focus**: Gaming GPUs are built to handle tasks like real-time rendering, texture mapping, and handling complex graphical effects (like ray tracing).
- **VRAM and Cooling**: While gaming GPUs often have less VRAM than their professional counterparts, they still come equipped with ample memory (usually 6GB to 24GB) to run the latest titles at high resolutions. Efficient cooling systems are also a priority for maintaining performance during long gaming sessions.
- **Price vs. Performance**: Gaming GPUs typically offer a better price-to-performance ratio than professional GPUs, making them a popular choice for hobbyists and casual gamers. However, their primary focus remains on delivering smooth, high-quality graphics for gaming, with secondary support for tasks like video editing and content creation.

Popular Gaming GPUs:

- **NVIDIA GeForce RTX 3090**: Top-tier performance for 4K gaming and VR, also capable of handling demanding workloads like 3D rendering and AI tasks.
- **AMD Radeon RX 6800 XT**: Offers excellent 1440p and 4K gaming performance with strong value for money.
- **NVIDIA GeForce RTX 3070**: A solid mid-range GPU that delivers great 1440p performance and supports ray tracing for high-quality gaming.

Professional GPUs

Professional GPUs, also known as **workstation GPUs**, are designed for tasks that require more than just gaming performance. These GPUs are tailored for industries such as 3D rendering, video editing, CAD (computer-aided design), scientific simulations, and machine learning. Unlike gaming GPUs, professional GPUs are optimized for stability, accuracy, and performance in resource-intensive applications.

- **Optimized for Compute**: Professional GPUs are designed for parallel computing and complex calculations. They are used in industries where high levels of precision, computational power, and data integrity are crucial. These GPUs excel in tasks like scientific simulations, AI training, deep learning, and rendering.

- **Memory Capacity and Error Correction**: Professional GPUs often come with more VRAM and support error-correcting code (ECC) memory, which ensures that computational errors are minimized—something that's vital in research and engineering environments.
- **Certifications and Support**: Professional GPUs often come with certified drivers and software optimizations for applications like AutoCAD, Maya, and SolidWorks. These certifications ensure that the hardware works seamlessly with the most popular industry-specific software, offering the best performance and stability.

Popular Professional GPUs:

- **NVIDIA Quadro RTX 8000**: A high-end professional GPU with 48GB of GDDR6 VRAM, designed for heavy-duty 3D rendering, scientific computing, and AI workloads.

- **AMD Radeon Pro VII**: Targeted at professionals who need robust performance for content creation, video editing, and scientific computing with 16GB of VRAM.
- **NVIDIA A100**: Specifically designed for data scientists, AI researchers, and machine learning applications, this card offers exceptional performance in deep learning and high-performance computing tasks.

Key Differences Between Gaming and Professional GPUs

Aspect	Gaming GPUs	Professional GPUs
Target Use Case	Gaming, casual content creation	CAD, 3D rendering, machine learning, simulations
Optimized For	Real-time rendering,	Precision, parallel computing,

	gaming graphics	scientific workloads
Memory (VRAM)	6GB - 24GB	16GB - 48GB
Cooling Systems	High-perform ance cooling for extended gaming	Advanced cooling for workstation reliability
Price	More affordable, better price-to-perfor mance	Higher price, often with specialized features
Error Correction	Not supported	ECC memory support for error-free calculations

Driver Support	Gaming-oriented drivers, some content creation support	Certified drivers for professional software
Performance	Best for gaming performance at various resolutions	Best for heavy-duty computing tasks, rendering, and simulations

When to Choose a Gaming GPU vs. a Professional GPU?

- **Choose a Gaming GPU** if you are primarily focused on gaming or casual content creation (e.g., video editing, 3D modeling). Gaming GPUs offer excellent value for money, providing high performance at a more affordable price. They are also versatile enough for other tasks like media consumption and light workloads.
- **Choose a Professional GPU** if you are working in industries that require high

accuracy, stability, and power for resource-heavy tasks. These tasks might include video editing at 8K resolutions, 3D rendering, architectural visualization, AI research, or scientific simulations. Professional GPUs are built to handle these workloads with the reliability and precision required for these specialized applications.

Tips for Building a Custom PC

Building a custom PC can be an exciting and rewarding project, whether you're looking to create a high-performance gaming machine, a workstation for professional tasks, or a general-purpose PC. By selecting the right components and assembling them yourself, you can tailor the system to your specific needs and budget. Here are some tips to help you build a custom PC:

1. Plan Your Build Around Your Purpose

Before purchasing any components, determine the purpose of your custom PC. Are you building a gaming rig, a workstation for 3D rendering, or a server for machine learning? Each purpose requires specific components, so be clear about your goals:

- **Gaming PC**: Focus on a powerful GPU, a fast CPU, and enough RAM to handle modern gaming. An SSD is also essential for quick load times.
- **Workstation for Professional Use**: Focus on a high-end GPU, a powerful multi-core CPU, plenty of RAM, and additional storage options (such as a large SSD for fast read/write speeds and a hard drive for mass storage).
- **General-purpose PC**: Aim for balanced components that provide a good combination of performance and cost-efficiency.

2. Choose the Right CPU

The CPU (Central Processing Unit) is the heart of your PC, so selecting the right one is crucial. The CPU dictates the overall performance of your system, particularly in tasks like gaming, video editing, or simulations. When building a custom PC, consider:

- **Gaming**: An Intel Core i5 or AMD Ryzen 5 is sufficient for most modern games. If you're gaming at higher resolutions or want better future-proofing, consider stepping up to an Intel Core i7 or AMD Ryzen 7.

- **Professional Use**: For tasks like 3D rendering, video editing, and other heavy workloads, consider high-end CPUs like the Intel Core i9 or AMD Ryzen 9 for multi-threaded performance.

3. Selecting the GPU

As discussed earlier, the GPU plays a crucial role in rendering graphics, whether for gaming or professional use. Based on your needs, select a GPU that suits your requirements:

- **Gaming**: A high-end GPU like the NVIDIA RTX 3080 or AMD Radeon RX 6800 will give you excellent performance at 1440p or 4K.
- **Professional Workstation**: Opt for a professional GPU like the NVIDIA Quadro RTX series for tasks that require precision and stability.

4. Memory (RAM)

RAM is essential for smooth multitasking and ensures that your CPU and GPU can efficiently handle multiple processes. For gaming, **16GB of RAM** is often sufficient, but for heavy professional tasks like video editing or 3D rendering, **32GB or more** is recommended.

5. Storage Options

Choose the right combination of storage devices:

- **SSD (Solid-State Drive)**: Crucial for fast boot times and load times, especially in gaming and professional applications.
- **HDD (Hard Disk Drive)**: Larger and more cost-effective, but slower. Great for mass storage, like video files or game libraries.

For optimal performance, consider installing your operating system and applications on an SSD while using an HDD for secondary storage.

6. Power Supply Unit (PSU)

The PSU provides power to all your components. Make sure you choose a PSU with enough wattage to support all your parts. A **650W to 750W PSU** is typically sufficient for most builds, but if you're using a high-end GPU or multiple storage devices, opt for a PSU with a higher wattage.

7. Cooling Systems

Efficient cooling is crucial, especially for gaming PCs and workstations with powerful GPUs and CPUs. You can choose from:

- **Air Cooling**: A simple and affordable option, ideal for most builds.
- **Liquid Cooling**: Offers superior cooling for high-end systems but comes at a higher price point.

Ensure your case has adequate airflow to maintain optimal temperatures for your components.

8. Build Quality and Compatibility

Make sure all your components are compatible with one another and fit into your chosen case. Check the **motherboard's size** (ATX, Micro-ATX, etc.), **GPU clearance**, and **RAM height** to ensure everything fits together without issues. Quality cases with good airflow, cable management options, and sturdy construction will help your PC last longer and stay cool under load.

Building a custom PC gives you control over every aspect of your system, allowing you to create a machine that fits your unique needs. By carefully selecting the right components and considering performance, cooling, and compatibility, you can ensure that your custom PC meets or exceeds your expectations.

Chapter 10: The Future of GPU Technology

Emerging Innovations in GPU Design

The world of GPU technology is evolving at an extraordinary pace, with continuous innovations that push the boundaries of what's possible in computing. As GPUs become increasingly integral to not only gaming but also scientific research, artificial intelligence (AI), and other advanced fields, the design of these powerful processors is also undergoing radical transformations.

One of the most significant innovations on the horizon is **3D stacking** of GPUs. Traditionally, GPUs have been built with flat, two-dimensional designs, but researchers are now exploring ways to stack multiple layers of processing units on top of each other. This **3D architecture** allows for faster data processing and improved performance, as it reduces the distance between the different parts of the GPU, improving data throughput. By stacking chips vertically, the size of the GPUs can be kept relatively compact while significantly increasing computational power.

Another emerging trend in GPU design is the adoption of **chiplet-based architectures**. Rather than relying on a single monolithic chip, chiplets are smaller, modular components that work together to form a larger GPU system. This modular approach allows for more efficient use of silicon, better performance scaling, and more flexibility in customization. It could be a game-changer for industries that require highly specialized GPU configurations, such as machine learning or autonomous driving.

Moreover, we are seeing the development of **quantum computing**-ready GPUs. Although quantum computing is still in its infancy, GPUs are being designed to work in tandem with quantum processors, enabling new forms of computing that harness the power of quantum mechanics. The **integration of quantum computing** with traditional GPU architecture could redefine everything from cryptography to AI research.

Finally, **AI-driven GPU design** is becoming a key factor in future innovations. Just as AI and machine learning have already revolutionized many fields, they are now being used to optimize the design of GPUs themselves. Machine learning algorithms can analyze vast amounts of data to determine the most efficient chip layouts, cooling methods, and power consumption strategies. By using AI to assist in the design process, we may see GPUs that are not only more powerful but also more energy-efficient and cost-effective.

How GPUs Will Shape Future Technologies

GPUs are no longer just the backbone of high-end gaming rigs—they are integral to numerous cutting-edge technologies that will shape the future. The massive parallel processing power of GPUs has made them ideal for solving complex problems in fields as diverse as **artificial intelligence**, **machine learning**, **medical research**, and **quantum computing**.

In the field of **artificial intelligence**, GPUs are already the cornerstone of deep learning and neural networks. As AI models become more advanced and data sets grow exponentially, the demand for more powerful GPUs will only increase. Future GPUs will likely incorporate **tensor processing cores** and other specialized hardware designed to accelerate AI training and inference. With the help of GPUs, AI will continue to evolve at an exponential rate, enabling advancements in autonomous vehicles, personalized healthcare, financial modeling, and much more.

In **scientific research**, GPUs will continue to power simulations that model everything from protein folding to climate change. The parallel architecture of GPUs makes them perfect for simulations that involve vast amounts of data, where traditional CPUs would struggle. Researchers are already using GPUs to simulate the behavior of complex molecules, design new drugs, and predict the effects of climate change on our planet. As GPUs become more advanced, they will play an even more crucial role in **big data analytics** and **quantum simulations**.

The rise of **virtual reality (VR)** and **augmented reality (AR)** technologies will also rely heavily on GPU advancements. These immersive technologies require immense computational power to render high-quality graphics in real time. GPUs will be essential in delivering lifelike environments and interactions for VR and AR applications, whether in gaming, training simulations, or entertainment. As **ray tracing** and other advanced rendering techniques become mainstream, GPUs will make VR and AR experiences more realistic and immersive than ever before.

Another area where GPUs will shape the future is **autonomous vehicles**. Self-driving cars rely on AI, sensor data, and high-speed processing to navigate the world around them. GPUs are already playing a vital role in processing data from cameras, radar, and lidar sensors in real time, allowing vehicles to make quick decisions and avoid obstacles. As self-driving technology advances, GPUs will be central to enabling fully autonomous transportation.

Finally, **blockchain and cryptocurrency** mining is an area where GPUs are already making an impact. The computational power required to mine cryptocurrencies like Bitcoin and Ethereum is enormous, and GPUs are more efficient than CPUs at handling the complex hash calculations necessary for mining. As the cryptocurrency industry grows, so will the demand for GPUs capable of performing these calculations faster and more efficiently.

Ethical Implications of GPU Advancements

While the future of GPU technology holds immense promise, it also raises several ethical questions that need to be addressed. As GPUs become more powerful and more integrated into everyday life, their potential to impact society—both positively and negatively—becomes increasingly significant.

One key concern is the **environmental impact** of GPU advancements. GPUs, especially high-performance models, consume a considerable amount of electricity and generate a lot of heat. As demand for more powerful GPUs grows, so too will the energy consumption of data centers, gaming rigs, and other devices that rely on these processors. The environmental cost of maintaining these systems could have long-term consequences, particularly as the world faces the challenges of climate change.

To mitigate this issue, manufacturers are focusing on improving the **energy efficiency** of GPUs. For example, new GPUs are being designed with better power management systems, lower thermal output, and more efficient manufacturing processes. However, there is still a long way to go before GPUs can be considered sustainable on a global scale.

Another ethical issue surrounding GPU advancements is their role in **surveillance and privacy**. With the ability to process large amounts of data in real time, GPUs can be used to power surveillance systems that track people's movements, monitor their activities, and even predict their behavior. While these technologies can have legitimate uses in law enforcement and security, they also raise concerns about privacy violations and the potential for misuse. Striking the right balance between security and privacy will be a critical challenge as GPU technology becomes more integrated into surveillance systems.

Moreover, **AI bias** is another concern. As GPUs continue to be used in training AI models, the data that is fed into these models can sometimes reflect societal biases, leading to unfair or discriminatory outcomes. Ensuring that AI systems are designed with fairness in mind—and that GPUs are used responsibly in their development—is a vital consideration in the ethical deployment of this technology.

Finally, as GPUs become increasingly powerful, they are also likely to become more expensive. The high cost of cutting-edge GPUs could create an inequality in access to powerful computing resources. This could limit the ability of individuals or smaller organizations to leverage the full potential of GPU-based technologies, exacerbating existing digital divides.

In conclusion, while GPUs hold the key to numerous breakthroughs across various industries, they also pose significant ethical challenges. From their environmental impact to their role in surveillance and AI development, it will be important for both the industry and society as a whole to address these concerns responsibly. By doing so, we can ensure that the future of GPU technology is one that benefits all of humanity, rather than exacerbating existing problems.

Conclusion

As we conclude this exploration of the powerful and intricate world of graphics processing units (GPUs), it's clear that these technological marvels are far more than just the heart of gaming systems. Throughout this book, we've uncovered the historical journey of GPUs, delved into their complex architecture, and explored their expanding influence beyond entertainment into fields such as artificial intelligence, scientific research, and autonomous technology.

The significance of GPUs in modern life cannot be overstated. These processors are at the core of a multitude of innovations, powering everything from immersive virtual worlds to groundbreaking medical simulations. Their ability to process vast amounts of data simultaneously has enabled new technologies to emerge, creating a profound impact on industries and societies alike. Whether it's revolutionizing gaming experiences or driving advancements in AI and machine learning, GPUs have become an indispensable force in shaping the digital age.

But what we've covered here is just the tip of the iceberg. GPU technology continues to evolve at an astonishing pace, and the future promises even more remarkable innovations. The cutting-edge designs on the horizon, such as quantum computing-ready GPUs and AI-driven chip development, will undoubtedly unlock new possibilities and transform industries in ways we can hardly imagine.

As you close this book, I encourage you to keep exploring the world of GPUs. Whether you're a curious enthusiast looking to dive deeper into the intricacies of graphics hardware, a professional aiming to stay ahead of the curve, or simply someone interested in understanding the technology that drives modern computing, the journey has only just begun. The GPU landscape is vast and constantly changing, with new advancements emerging every day. Continue to seek out knowledge, stay curious, and embrace the future of technology as it unfolds before our eyes